MW00446856

FORESTCORE
Coloring Book

chartwell books

Enter the
enchanted woods,

where *dappled light*
softly illuminates the
ferns, mushrooms, and tiny
creatures on forest floor.

This *magical world* is here
for you to color, inviting you
to discover the beauty of
wild flora and fauna.

Forestcore Coloring Book takes you to an untamed place where the pace slows and your cares melt away. Inspired by the popular interior design, fashion, and art trend, the forestcore aesthetic centers on natural beauty. Your creative side will ignite as you choose your palette for these drawings. Choose earthy greens and browns or go in a completely different direction. It's up to you.

Have you heard of forest bathing? It's the practice of going to a forest with intentionality, letting the beauty of nature offer restoration and rejuvenation. After breathing in the fresh air, listening to bird song, and letting the sun warm you, you'll release your worries. Those benefits can have a long-lasting effect. Even if you can't get to a forest in real life, these designs will take you there whenever you need that kind of quiet time to wind down. Pick up this coloring book before bed, during a break from work or any time you just need a few moments of creative me time.

You don't have to have artistic talent to enjoy this coloring book. *Unwind, experiment, and enjoy* your journey into a world of harmony and nature.

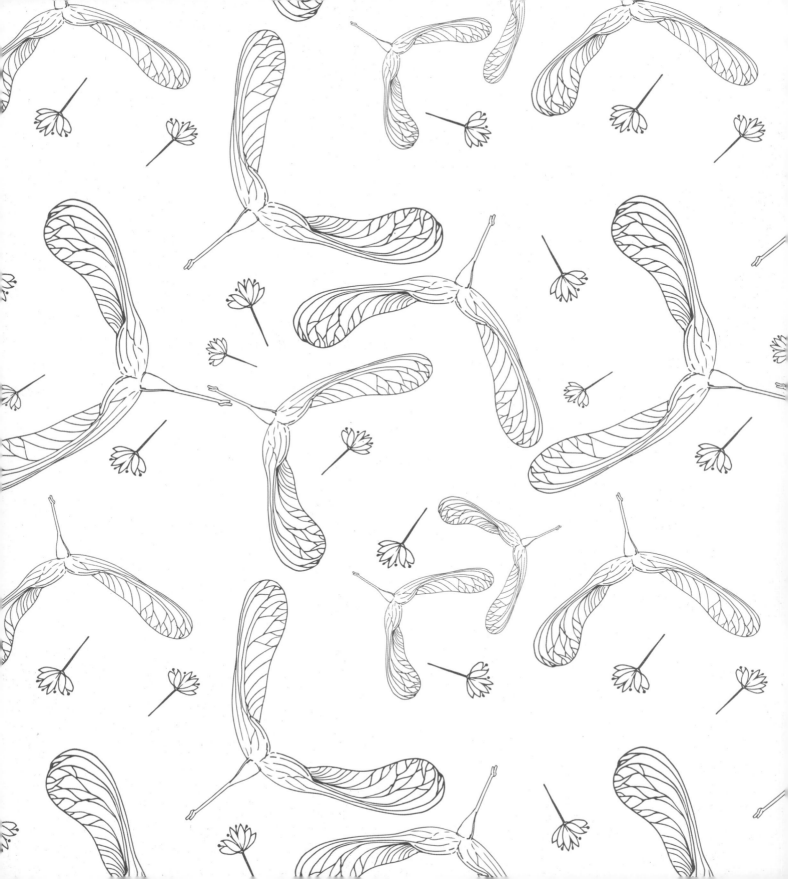

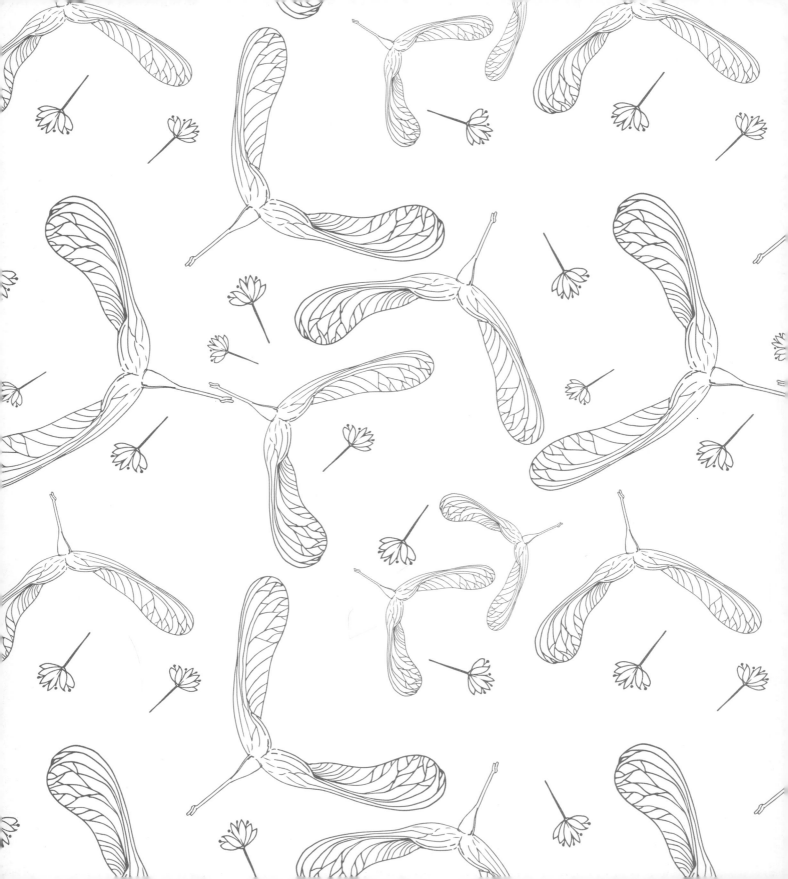

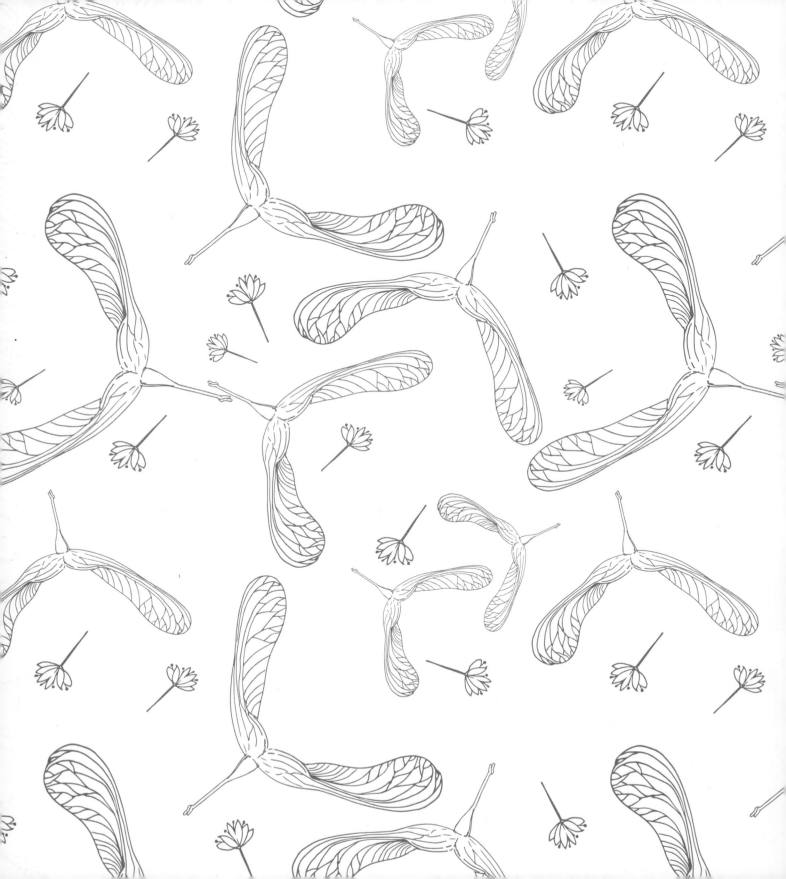

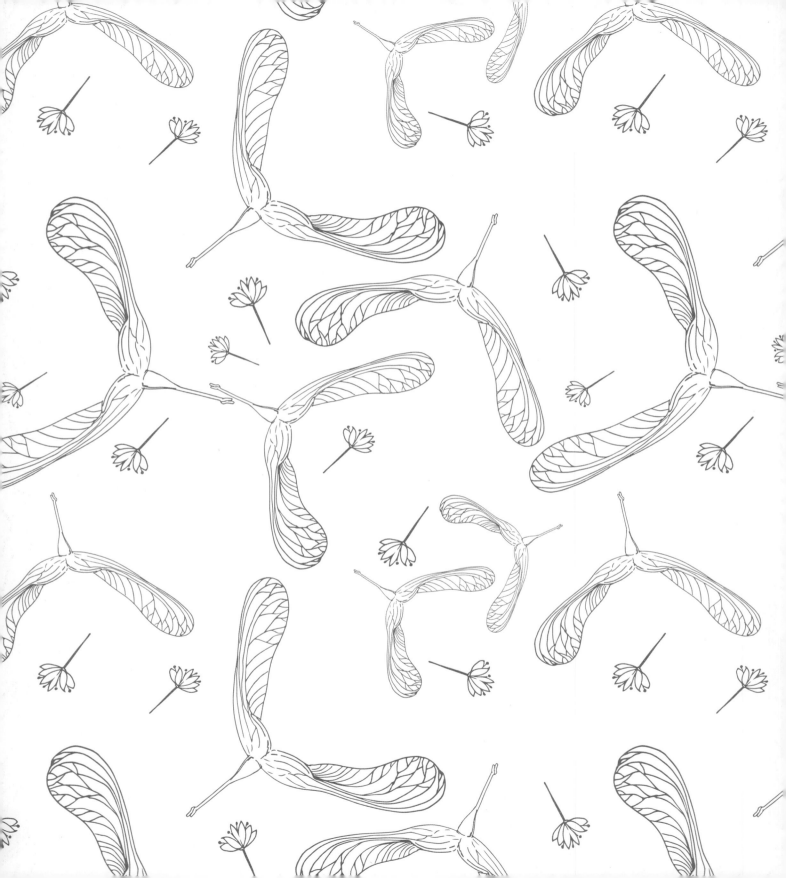

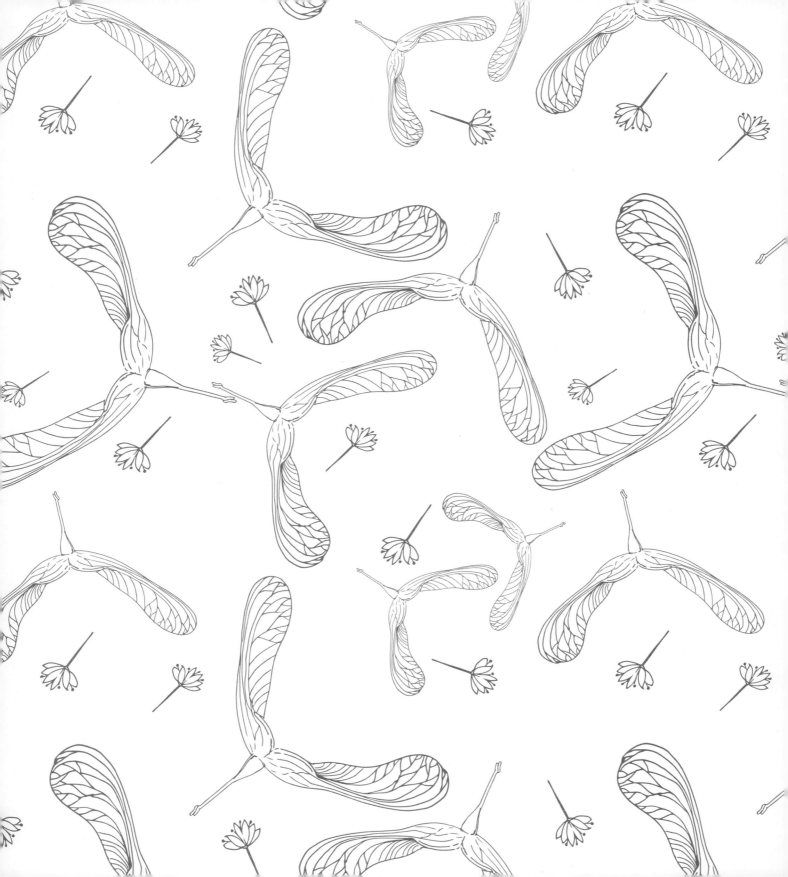

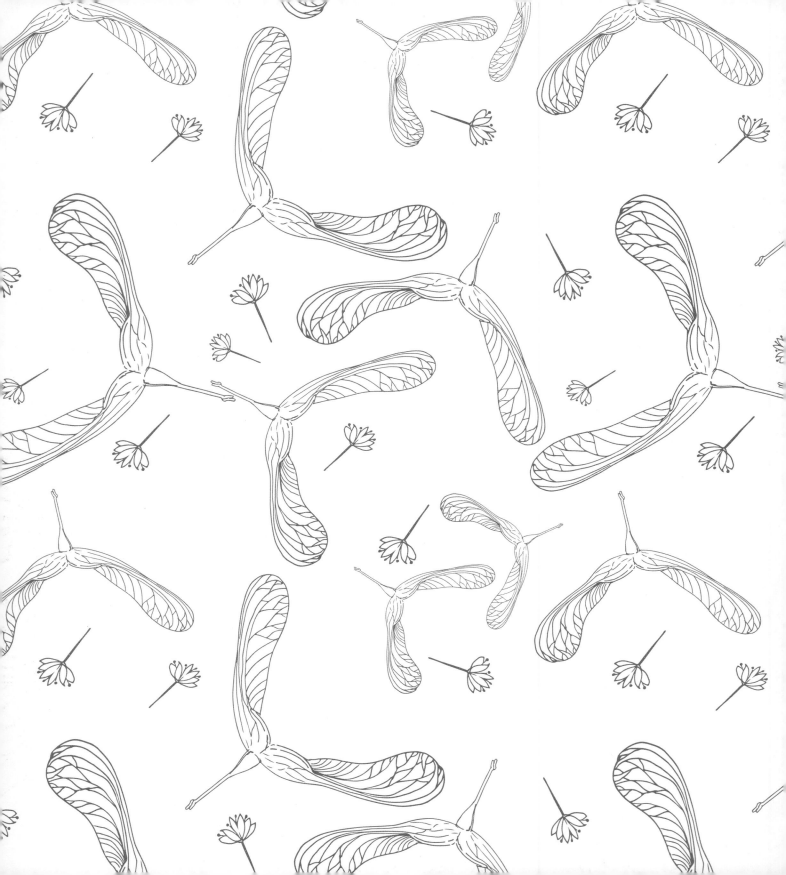

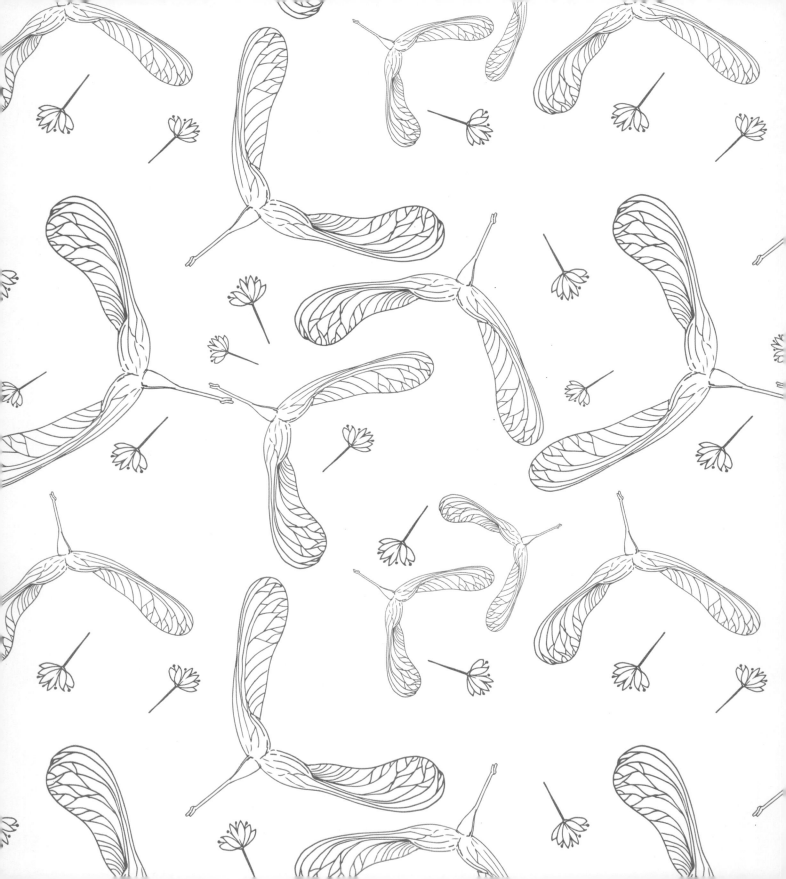

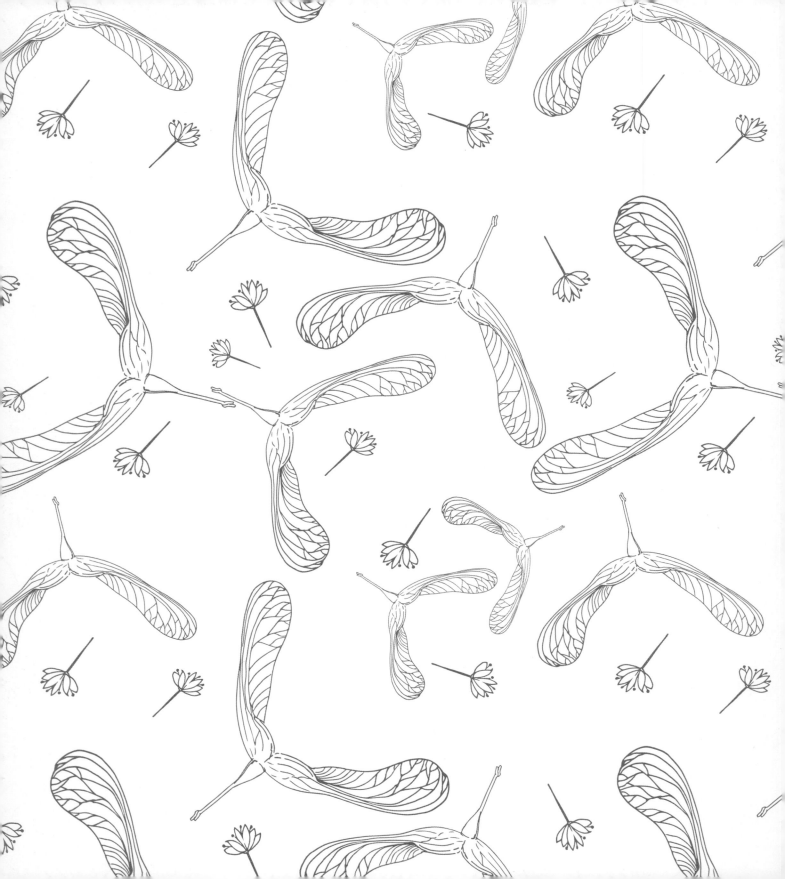

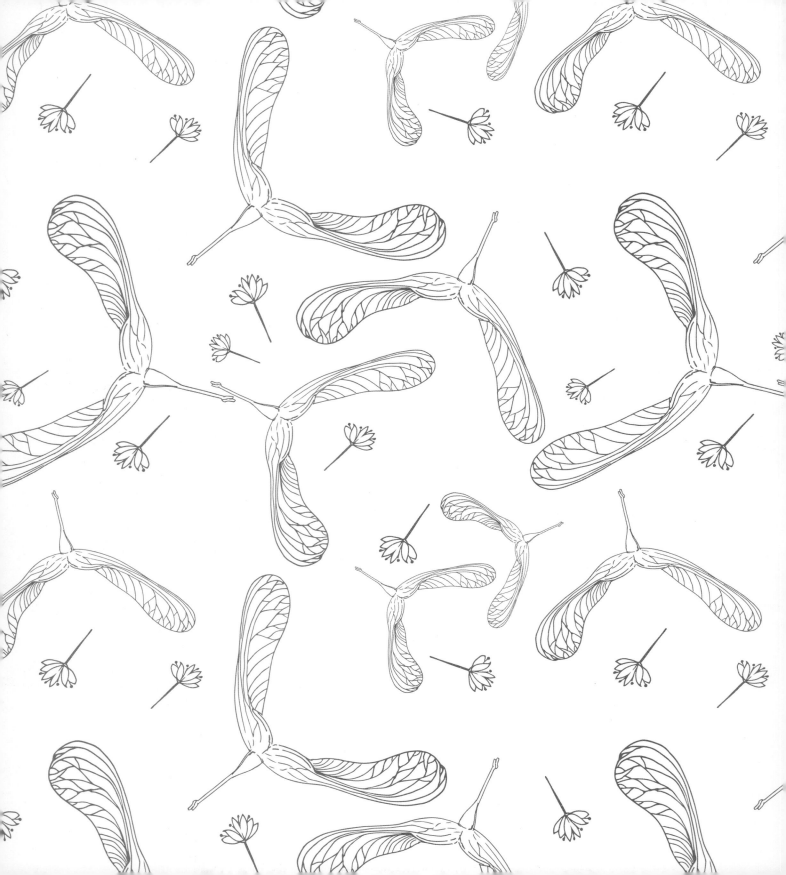

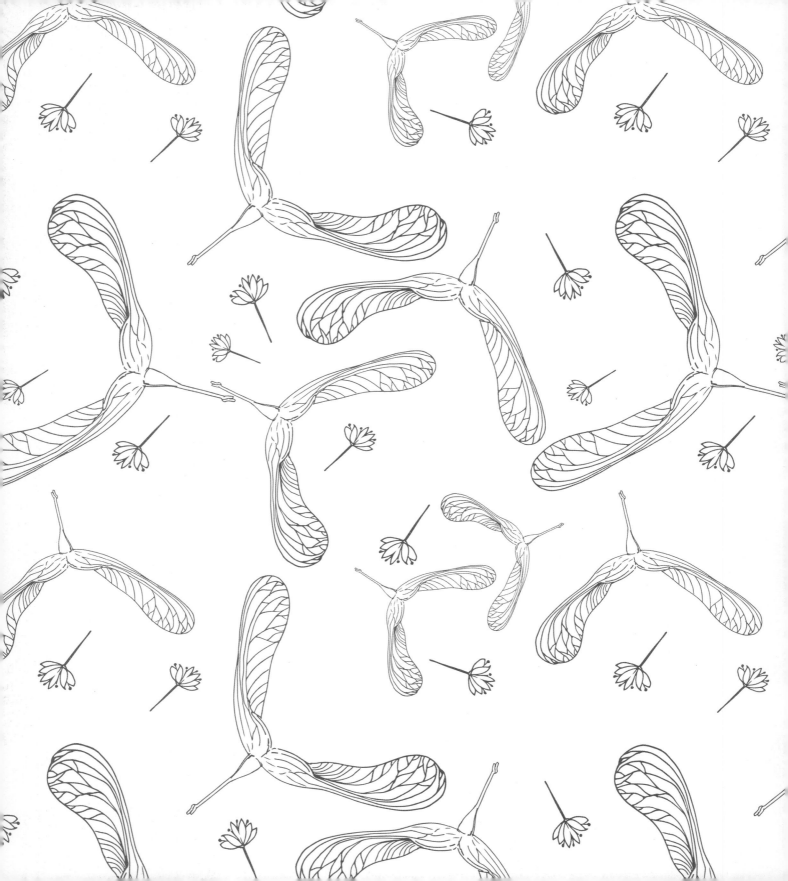

Quarto

© 2023 Quarto Publishing Group USA Inc.

This edition published in 2023 by Chartwell Books,
an imprint of The Quarto Group
142 West 36th Street, 4th Floor
New York, NY 10018 USA
T (212) 779-4972 F (212) 779-6058
www.Quarto.com

All rights reserved. No part of this book may be reproduced in any
form without written permission of the copyright owners. All images
in this book have been reproduced with the knowledge and prior
consent of the artists concerned, and no responsibility is accepted
by producer, publisher, or printer for any infringement of copyright or
otherwise, arising from the contents of this publication. Every effort has
been made to ensure that credits accurately comply with information
supplied. We apologize for any inaccuracies that may have occurred
and will resolve inaccurate or missing information in a subsequent
reprinting of the book.

10 9 8 7 6 5 4 3 2 1

Chartwell titles are also available at discount for retail, wholesale,
promotional, and bulk purchase. For details, contact the Special Sales
Manager by email at specialsales@quarto.com or by mail at The Quarto
Group, Attn: Special Sales Manager, 100 Cummings Center Suite 265D,
Beverly, MA 01915, USA.

ISBN: 978-0-7858-4335-1

Publisher: Wendy Friedman
Senior Publishing Manager: Meredith Mennitt
Senior Design Manager: Michael Caputo
Editor: Joanne O'Sullivan
Designer: Kate Sinclair

All stock design elements ©Shutterstock

Printed in China